ELT Development
Series

SERIES EDITOR Thomas S. C. Farrell

T0170755

REVISED EDITION

Teaching Speaking

Tasha Bleistein
Melissa K. Smith
Marilyn Lewis

tesol press

www.tesol.org/bookstore

TESOL International Association
1925 Ballenger Avenue
Alexandria, Virginia, 22314 USA
www.tesol.org

Director of Publishing and Product Development: Myrna Jacobs
Copy Editor: Meg Moss
Production Editor: Kari S. Dalton
Cover Design: Citrine Sky Design
Interior Design and Layout: Capitol Communications, LLC

The publications of the TESOL Press present a variety of viewpoints. The views expressed or implied in this publication, unless otherwise noted, should not be interpreted as official positions of the organization.

ISBN 9781945351921
eBook ISBN 9781945351938
Library of Congress Control Number 2019956818

Table of Contents

Series Editor's Preface

The *English Language Teacher Development (ELTD)* series consists of a set of short resource books for ESL/EFL teachers that are written in a jargon-free and accessible manner for all types of teachers of English (native, nonnative, experienced, and novice). The ELTD series is designed to offer teachers a theory-to-practice approach to second language teaching, and each book presents a wide variety of practical approaches to and methods of teaching the topic at hand. Each book also offers reflections to help teachers interact with the materials presented. The books can be used in preservice settings or in in-service courses and by individuals looking for ways to refresh their practice. Now, after nearly 10 years in print, the ELTD series presents newly updated, revised editions that are even more dynamic than their first editions. Each of these revised books has an expanded number of chapters, as well as updated references from which various activities have been drawn and lesson plans for teachers to consider.

Tasha Bleistein, Melissa K. Smith, and Marilyn Lewis' revised edition of *Teaching Speaking* again explores different approaches to how teachers can teach speaking in second language classrooms. They have updated the references and research, and added more reflective questions as well as new activities, charts and a detailed lesson plan for teachers to consider. They have also added a new chapter that explores how to use speaking to teach.

This revised edition is again a valuable addition to the literature in our profession.

I am very grateful to the authors of the ELTD series for sharing their knowledge and expertise with other TESOL professionals to make these short books affordable for all language teachers throughout the world. It is truly an honor for me to work again with each of these authors for the advancement of TESOL.

Thomas S. C. Farrell

CHAPTER 1

Introduction

For much of the history of English language teaching, speaking English was not the goal. Language was taught as an academic pursuit focused on reading, writing, or passing grammar-based exams. Because of the prominence of English in the world today and the changing needs of learners, English language learners are more motivated than ever to improve their communication skills.

What Is Speaking?

How would you explain speaking? Is it simply making sounds, or does an utterance need to be understood to be considered speaking? Take a moment to write down your own definition of speaking.

REFLECTIVE QUESTION

- Speaking is _____.

In your answer, maybe you included communicating aloud. Or maybe you mentioned that speaking is meaningful interaction between people using words.

With Whom Do People Speak?

With ever-increasing globalization, international communication is the focus for many English language learners. This has led to questions about what variety of English is "correct."

REFLECTIVE QUESTIONS

- Who should decide what type of English is spoken?

- How can you encourage students to accept varieties of English from around the world?

The idea that there are only two types of English, British and American, has been found faulty; one of the authors discovered this view from a child's remark when observing an English class in Mongolia. During the break, a young girl who heard her chatting with the teacher inquired about the author's home country. After pointing to New Zealand on the map, the girl exclaimed, "Oh! But you sound quite educated." Authentic, or "real," English is not only the English spoken in the United States, but is also the English spoken in countries such as Chad, Chile, and China. Teachers of English are encouraged to draw on and celebrate the rich and diverse varieties of the language used around the world today (Alsagoff, McKay, Hu, & Renandya, 2012; Jenkins, 2006).

In This Book

To meet the needs of students, teachers of oral English have three main tasks: (1) discover how speaking works, (2) look for ways to introduce students to the language of conversation, and (3) provide students with opportunities to practice speaking English. This book aims to prepare teachers for these three tasks.

Chapters 2 and 3 examine how speaking works through learning what it means to be a communicatively competent speaker of a second language (L2). Chapter 2 focuses on linguistic and discourse competence and specifically covers language forms and how to put those together into conversational contexts. Chapter 3 addresses sociocultural and strategic competence, looking at how to carry on a conversation appropriately and successfully despite cultural differences and language barriers.

The final four chapters move from theory to classroom application, exploring different approaches to designing speaking activities and lesson plans (chapter 4), using speaking to teach content (chapter 5), describing some of the challenges inherent in the teaching of speaking in different contexts (chapter 6), and enhancing students' learning outside of class and assessing speaking (chapter 7).

CHAPTER 2

Language Forms in Conversational Contexts

Some people learning to speak a new language find it difficult to get words out of their mouth, although what comes out is accurate; for others, the words come out and even flow somewhat, but these speakers make many mistakes.

REFLECTIVE QUESTIONS

● As a language student, what aspects of speaking an L2 (such as vocabulary, pronunciation, or organizing your ideas) did you find most difficult? Did your classmates struggle in the same area?

● What aspects of speaking do your current students struggle with? How do they differ from your own?

Communicative Competence

In the next two chapters, we will examine what communicative competence is and how it relates to the teaching of speaking. Communicative language teaching (CLT) was developed decades ago to emphasize the importance of using spoken and written language for real-world communication. Critics observed that some teachers took no notice of accuracy in language, although CLT does include a focus on grammar. In fact, its intention was to include all aspects of communicative competence, which, according to Canale and Swain (1980), includes vocabulary learning (lexis), sentence structure (syntax), the meaning of words (semantics), and sounds (phonology) of a language.

In addition to linguistic competence, other aspects of communicative competence include discourse competence (whether speech is coherent and cohesive), sociolinguistic competence (whether language is appropriate to the context), and strategic competence (whether a speaker can repair a conversation when it starts to break down).

The following sections explore two aspects of learning to speak: language forms (linguistic competence) and how to put language together into the context of conversations (discourse competence).

Language Forms

In the past, popular methods of language teaching (such as the grammar translation method) primarily focused on accuracy of language. In many classrooms, the focus of English study is still mastery of grammar or vocabulary with little emphasis on communication. When people take part in conversations, however, they do not have time to consult a dictionary and correct their language. CLT emphasizes real-world speaking by preparing students not only to study English as an academic task, but also to use it in conversations. Studying language communicatively results in well-developed grammar knowledge as well as better communication skills (Savignon, 2005).

Fluency and Accuracy

Although the focus of CLT is to allow students to use the language fluently, this does not preclude activities intended to improve accuracy. After all, fluency without some level of accuracy is not fluency at all.

On the other hand, simply focusing on accuracy will not necessarily lead to fluency.

REFLECTIVE QUESTIONS

- Which do you think is more important, fluency or accuracy? Should teachers focus more on one or the other in a speaking class?

Depending on the focus of an activity or lesson, the primary goal may be fluency, accuracy, or a combination of the two. Arevart and Nation (1991) found that fluency and accuracy may both improve at the same time. In conducting a 4–3–2 activity (see Table 2.1) generally associated with fluency, they found that students' fluency and accuracy both improved.

Fluency can be encouraged when teachers

- use material that is familiar to learners, such as grammar or vocabulary they have already learned;

- use repetition so students repeat an activity or use the same language again in a similar context; and

- apply some pressure on students (not enough to make them unduly nervous) to perform the task slightly faster than normal.

In environments where students do not have easy access to English outside of the classroom, more time may need to be spent in class on fluency activities. A number of classroom activities that improve fluency are included in Table 2.1 as well as in subsequent chapters.

Table 2.1. Activities to Promote Fluency

Activity	Explanation
4–3–2	Students work in pairs and present information or a story to a partner. The first round, the student has 4 minutes to complete his or her turn. The second round allows 3 minutes, and the final round 2. The student shares the same information during each round but in a shorter amount of time. This activity can be adapted for lower-level students who struggle to speak for four minutes by reducing the time for each round and can be more engaging if partners switch for each round.
Improving recordings	Students describe a picture or answer a question while recording, then listen to the recording and note areas where improvements are needed. Students continue to rerecord until they are satisfied.
Rehearsed speeches	Students prepare a talk alone and then either record themselves and self-evaluate or practice with classmates before presentation in front of a larger group, such as the entire class.
Consensus building	Students must come to an agreement that involves compromise or negotiation. It may be a problem-solving activity or a ranking activity (e.g., which candidates should be selected for jobs out of the provided applications).

Adapted from Nation and Newton (2009) and Bohlke (2014).

Most English teachers agree that fluency is as important as accuracy in authentic communication. Letting students know which parts of the lesson involve answering correctly and which parts are to practice conveying one's message using a range of communication strategies helps them to note different foci during activities. Remind students that making mistakes is part of the language acquisition process, and make it clear when you will focus on error correction and when you want students to use the language they have.

REFLECTIVE QUESTIONS

- How can you assure students that making mistakes is part of the language learning process?

- Do any cultural barriers to fluency or accuracy Activities exist in your context?

Corrective Feedback

Related to the discussion of fluency and accuracy is error correction in the speaking classroom. Students who are experimenting with a new language will make mistakes. They are using their interlanguage (Selinker, 1972), their personal language that combines features from both their first language (L1) and their second (L2).

Teachers aim to find the balance between too little and too much feedback on student errors. An abundance of error feedback can cause students to stop trying to communicate. At the other end of the spectrum, too little can lead to students' assuming that an error is correct.

One way to balance the amount of feedback is to focus only on global errors, or those that affect understanding (Hendrickson, 1980). If the goal is to help students to be intelligible, you can use this as a guide for when to give error correction: Does the error affect intelligibility or make it so the listener cannot understand the intended meaning? Another option is to focus on errors that have recently been the topic of instruction.

Error correction can be given in ways that do not humiliate learners. For example, you can address common errors to the whole class and not target one student. You can also create a classroom environment where errors are viewed as common and expected aspects of language learning and the correction of errors is part of the regular learning process. If students understand that you are helping by providing respectful feedback, then they will hopefully view errors and feedback more positively.

Lyster, Saito, and Sato (2013) organized corrective feedback types into either *reformulations*, where the teacher gives the correct utterance to the student, or *prompts*, where the teacher elicits the correction from the students. Each of these may be either implicit or explicit. See Table 2.2

Many teachers will combine more than one form of error feedback. For example, a teacher might repeat the error and then correct the error.

REFLECTIVE QUESTIONS

- What type of feedback on errors do you think is most effective?
- How do you generally respond to student errors?

Table 2.2. Feedback Types

	Implicit	Explicit
Reformulations	*Conversational recasts:* Restating the utterance in conversation, generally when communication breaks down **Example** Student: I ate sandpot for my lunch. Teacher: So you had a pot of soup for lunch.	*Didactic recasts:* Restating the utterance when communication is not impacted **Example** Student: I borrow him a stapler. Teacher: You lent him the stapler. *Explicit correction:* Clearly indicating an error and restating **Example** Student: I eat salad yesterday. Teacher: Not *eat*. I *ate* salad yesterday. *Explicit correction with metalinguistic explanation:* Error identified and rules included **Example** Student: I twenty-six. Teacher: Every sentence needs a verb. We need the "be verb." I am twenty-six.

continued on next page

Table 2.2 Feedback Types *(continued)*

	Implicit	Explicit
Prompts	*Repetition:* Repeating the student's error, generally with emphasis on the area in need of correction **Example** Student: I need go to the store. Teacher: I *need go* to the store. *Clarification request:* Asking the speaker to repeat or explain **Example** Student: [Unintelligible] Teacher: Could you repeat that?	*Metalinguistic clue:* A prompt provided by the teacher for the student to self-correct **Example** Student: I buyed three tacos. Teacher: What is the irregular past tense for *buy*? **Elicitation:** Asking student to provide the correction **Example** Student: I am /b/ery ('bɛri) hungry. Teacher: Places two front teeth on bottom lip and points to mouth as a reminder of the pronunciation of /v/ And asks, "Can you repeat *very*?"

Lyster and Ranta (1997) found that teachers use recasts most often, although subsequent research shows that this varies depending on the teacher and the setting (Sheen & Ellis, 2011). Uptake is how students respond to the error correction by indicating in some way that they can correct the error. Although the teachers in the Lyster and Ranta study most commonly used recasts, student uptake was least likely to occur with recasts. Elicitations and metalinguistic feedback led to greater uptake among students. With the research somewhat contradictory, the best approach may be to provide a variety of feedback types to students (Lightbown & Spada, 2013).

Consider recording your class or having someone observe how you give feedback to students. You might be surprised by how and when you give feedback. Sheen and Ellis (2011) offer some suggestions based on research on corrective feedback:

- Generally, learners want to be corrected, and correction promotes language acquisition.

- Effective feedback may be given immediately after an error or later.

- The most effective feedback is explicit (learners know they are being corrected) and asks students to produce language.

- Learner self-correction seems to lead to the greatest learning.

Finally, remember that error feedback should be balanced with positive feedback.

Form-Focused Instruction

Focusing on form (or grammar) in language is enfcouraged even in a communicative speaking classroom. Lightbown and Spada (2013) define *form-focused instruction* (FFI) as "instruction that draws attention to the form and structures of the language within the context of communicative interaction" (p. 218).

In FFI, there are further divisions (see Figure 2.1 and chapter 4).

1. Teaching forms when they arise in a lesson (*focus on form*): For example, a lesson on food might involve an unplanned minilesson on quantifiers (e.g., *all*, *some*).

2. Paying attention to forms outside of communicative interaction (*focus on forms*): For example, the teacher plans the forms that will be taught before the class begins.

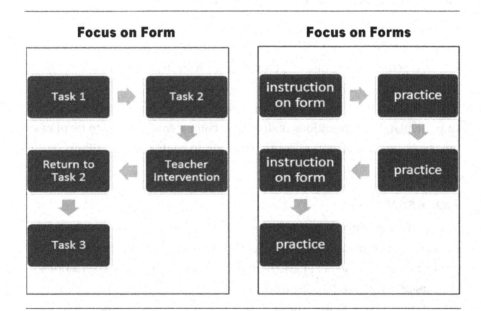

Figure 2.1. Difference Between Focus on Form and Focus on Forms

Discourse Competence

One of the unwritten rules of conversation is that the words must flow. If they do not, the talk is ineffective. In other words, language forms must be put together into phrases that join into conversations that flow, change direction, and grow or shrink as people drop in and out.

Teachers can help their students understand what makes a conversation, in particular, the conventions of discourse competence, or how to tie phrases and sentences into strings of communication in context so that others understand the meaning.

Cohesion

The term for joining ideas in writing or in speech is *cohesion*. In writing, cohesion means making one sentence flow to the next sentence and one paragraph flow to the next paragraph (Christiansen, 2011). Conversations flow smoothly when speakers link their ideas with what has been said just previously. In other words, they use cohesive devices to tie phrases and sentences together, and they make connections even when switching from one speaker to another. Still, conversations are messy and sometimes do not flow smoothly, even when people are using their L1.

Teaching Discourse

The goal in teaching discourse competence is to help students make conversations flow and understand how to string ideas together with cohesive devices or other features.

Cohesive Devices

One way to help students make ideas flow is to use cohesive devices, which act like glue sticking the parts of a conversation together. For example, to add information, speakers can use words or phrases such as *and*, *what's more*, and *also*. To describe a series of events, speakers might use words such as *first*, *next*, or *finally*.

Repetition

People repeat themselves to keep ideas flowing, perhaps starting with phrases such as *Once again* or *As I was saying*. Sometimes speakers do this after an interruption, when people do not seem to be listening, or just to make a point more strongly, either in the same or different words. Repetition keeps both listeners and speakers on track. Teachers can help learners understand that repetition is natural and useful when using English.

Reference Words

In conversations, people do not keep repeating the key words, those that hold meaning. Instead, they use reference words such as *there* or *this*. For example, imagine walking into a room and hearing the following utterances:

A: Yes. Believe me. I was there.

B: Really? How long were you there?

Although you may have no idea what the speakers are talking about, they do, and their use of *there* makes the conversation flow more smoothly. Imagine what it would sound like otherwise:

A: Yes. Believe me. I was at the Teaching English to Speakers of Other Languages conference.

B: Really? How long were you at the conference on Teaching English to Speakers of Other Languages?

Taking the Floor

To keep the flow of conversation going, sometimes speakers begin their turns (or take the floor) by referring to what someone else has said. For example, when people are sharing opinions, they might begin their turns with transitions such as *I see what you're saying, but. . . .* Or when they want to describe a similar experience, they might say *The same thing happened to me. . . .*

Yielding the Floor

Keeping the conversation flowing sometimes involves giving other people a turn or keeping them talking. When people want to draw someone else into a conversation, they might ask questions such as *What do you think?* or *You were there too, weren't you?* To keep another person talking, a speaker can also ask questions or make comments that show interest. The questions need not be very clever and sometimes can simply repeat the person's words. Look at the following examples. The first yields the floor with a question. In the second, B's repetition with questioning intonation invites A to continue speaking and keeps the conversation flowing.

A: The concert was amazing. You could really feel the majesty of the music. . . . Isn't that how you felt too?

B: It is, although I'm not sure I felt it quite as strongly as you did.

A: Then I really did get a shock.

B: You got a shock?

REFLECTIVE QUESTIONS

- Do you use these strategies in your own conversations?

- How can you help students add these devices to their English conversation skills

Conclusion

Learning to speak involves gaining some mastery over the forms of language (linguistic competence) and stringing those forms together into conversations (discourse competence). Success in speaking includes being able to speak accurately and fluently within the flow of conversational contexts. Yet, the learning process does not stop here.

CHAPTER 3

Conversations in Real-World Contexts

A U.S. university department referred a visiting scholar to the intensive English program because he was having trouble communicating. When the program assessed his language, both his written and oral English levels were above the highest level offered by the program. What was the problem, then? Although his English was completely understandable, people were offended by his manner of communication.

Once people learn relevant forms and how to put them together into conversational contexts, have they fully learned how to speak the language? No. Like the visiting scholar, they still need to figure out how to communicate in real-world contexts. Doing so involves two elements: how to communicate politely and appropriately in the world beyond the classroom (sociocultural competence) and being aware of strengths and weaknesses, and learning how to overcome weaknesses or navigate communication breakdown (strategic competence).

Sociocultural Competence

Conversation is often made up of a series of speech acts or language functions. For example, perhaps you borrowed (using a speech act) a book from a colleague and accidentally spilled tea on it. If so, you will probably apologize, and your colleague will forgive you (both apologizing and forgiving are speech acts). Then, you might talk about what you have read, using any number of speech acts such as sharing ideas or opinions or agreeing or disagreeing. Finally, you might close the conversation by expressing gratitude for the conversation or loan of the book and definitely by saying goodbye.

REFLECTIVE QUESTIONS

- Look at an English textbook.
  - — Can you identify different speech acts or functions in lessons?
  - — Is there instruction on how to use the speech acts appropriately or how to change one's speech to make it more polite based on context?

Politeness

Politeness is difficult to define because it varies from one language group to another and even within groups that speak the same language.

REFLECTIVE QUESTIONS

- Consider the following generalizations. Do you agree or disagree with them? Why?
  - — Speaking honestly when you feel critical of someone is more polite than pretending you like their behavior.
  - — If you want someone to do something for you at work, it is more polite to make a vague suggestion than to tell them directly to do it.
  - — When you want to turn down an invitation, it is more polite to tell a white lie than to say *No, thank you.*

You probably found yourself responding to some of these statements with the thought *It depends* . . . . That is the problem with trying to make up rules of politeness: They are not the same among all groups of people because of different politeness factors.

Politeness Factors

Some words, phrases, or ways of speaking are out of place in one context but not in another. When teaching learners how to communicate appropriately, teachers need to help them consider the factors affecting their choices and how those factors influence politeness.

Society

The rules of society (the cultural norms) influence how polite people should behave in certain situations. For example, some societies require more power distance (Hofstede, 1980) between those in authority and their subordinates. Thus, you will see more politeness expressed between a worker and a boss or between someone younger and someone older.

Situation

The situation also influences the choices speakers make. In particular, the level of formality influences the way they speak. For example, the way people communicate over a meal in their home may differ from their communication at a formal dinner. The seriousness of the situation may also affect ways of communicating; borrowing your friend's book is not the same as borrowing a large sum of money. The second situation may require a higher level of politeness. Finally, the effect the situation has on the listener may influence the speaker's choices. Offering more chocolate usually has a positive effect. Asking someone to help carry a heavy box may have a negative effect and so requires more politeness.

Relationship

The choices speakers make are influenced by the people they are talking to, the closeness of the relationship, and the authority, power, or status of anyone involved. For example, the choices a group of young people might make when talking to each other may not be the same as when they are speaking with their grandparents. How someone communicates with a coworker may differ from talking with a boss, and parents may speak one way with children and another with each other.

Script

As people participate in conversational situations like those described, they follow patterns from a script (Yule, 1996; Mey, 2001). Like the script for a play, a conversation script tells people what to say. Unlike a play script, though, it gives people choices for how to talk: a selection of words, phrases, and ways (including nonverbal ways) to perform speech acts and engage in conversation. How people make these choices depends on sociocultural competence, which tells speakers what selections from the script are appropriate in particular situations in specific societies and cultures. In other words, scripts guide speakers to communicate politely.

How the Factors Work Together

As Figure 3.1 shows, each politeness factor depends on others. Within a particular society, people cannot decide what level of politeness to use in a situation without also thinking about relationships. Thus, when returning the tea-stained book (see the earlier example), your apology to a colleague who is also a close friend may differ from the one you give to someone to whom you are not as close. Add authority to the relationship—for instance, if the book belongs to your boss—and the level of politeness may change again. Change the seriousness of the situation—for instance, if you borrowed and wrecked your boss's car—and the level of politeness changes yet again.

You can help students understand how the politeness factors work together. Questions such as those in the following Reflective Question might help.

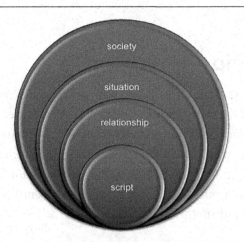

Figure 3.1. Politeness Factors Diagram

REFLECTIVE QUESTIONS

Questions to consider regarding politeness:

- What relationship do I have with the person I am talking to?
  - How close is our relationship?
  - Who, if anyone, has authority, power, or status in the relationship?

- What situation are we in?
  - How formal or informal is it?
  - How serious is it?
  - What effect is it having on the person I am talking to?

- What does society say is appropriate and polite in this situation given my relationship with this person?

Teaching Politeness

Teachers need to help learners make wise choices from conversation scripts that enable them to act appropriately and politely in different relationships and situations in a particular society. Should teachers make a list of forbidden words? That is impossible, as demonstrated by the example in the Reflective Questions from an English language class made up of immigrants in the United States.

REFLECTIVE QUESTIONS

A teacher overheard one of her students using a swear word during a group conversation task.

Teacher: I think you will find people do not use that word when they are trying to be polite.

Student: But the women at work use it all the time.

- What was the misunderstanding here? After all, the student was speaking in a way she heard used around her all day. The teacher, on the other hand, had different contexts in mind.

- What advice would you give to the teacher in this situation?

When the teacher thought about this incident later, she decided that she should give different advice to her students. She advised

- listen to and imitate the people you want to sound like,

- notice differences in the way different groups of people talk, and

- find out what parents teach their children about words that are not polite.

In addition to this teacher's advice, you may want to help learners understand how to mitigate, or soften, their language when situations and relationships call for more politeness. As the preceding example shows, word choice may be one way to soften language. Some possible ways are listed in Table 3.1.

Table 3.1. Mitigation of Language

Method	Less Polite	More Polite or Softened
Word choice	*That idea makes no sense.*	*That idea is a little confusing.*
Sentence structure	*Give me that booklet.*	*Would you mind if I borrowed your booklet?*
Apology or excuse	*How old are you?*	*I know I'm not supposed to ask this, but I'm really curious. How old are you?*
Indirect language	*You got a haircut. I don't like it.*	*You got a haircut. Wow! It's really different.*
Nonverbal cues	*I disagree!*	Said quietly and gently, with a smile: *I disagree.*

Helping learners communicate politely is more than simply teaching them rules. They need to be able to make wise choices on their own. Here are some things that may help:

- Exposure to authentic language: Think about how you could bring authentic language, for example, from television or movies, into the classroom or make use of any opportunities your students have to hear English outside the classroom.

- Talking about politeness: Have students analyze how politeness works by providing case studies to discuss how language should be used between people in particular situations.

- Practice: Talking about how to be polite is one thing, but actually doing it is another; role-playing is a good way for students to practice making wise choices in real conversations.

Strategic Competence

As people often experience, even when they have learned how to speak in real-world conversations, communication can still break down or stop, and sometimes they do not even know why. Those who want to keep talking do not just walk away thinking that it is too hard or fatiguing. Rather, they try to identify the problem and then find a way around it. Strategic competence consists of developing an awareness of your strengths and weaknesses and finding ways to make yourself understood with words or body language. Brown defined strategic competence as, "The ability to use verbal and nonverbal communicative techniques to compensate for breakdowns in communication or insufficient competence. It includes the ability to make 'repairs' and to sustain communication . . . "(2014, p. 208). Developing skills to repair conversation can help English language learners feel more confident and competent in speaking because they are equipped to deal with hurdles they encounter. Following are some strategies to help students deal with communication breakdowns:

- Ask the meaning of a word.
- Ask if your understanding is correct.
- Ask the speaker to repeat or slow down.
- Guess.
- Give an example.
- Spell out a word or ask someone else to.
- Use facial expression to show confusion.
- Use nonverbal or visual cues to express meaning.

The following sections offer some additional strategies to teach students to maintain conversations.

Circumlocution or Paraphrasing

Circumlocution involves using several words—instead of the one word you do not know—to communicate something. One way is to explain. Even in their L1, speakers explain when they are trying to communicate something beyond their own level of knowledge. For example, often someone wanting to convey a computer problem to a technician on the phone will use nontechnical language.

> A: Just a minute ago when I was typing, one of those little icons disappeared.
>
> B: Which one?
>
> A: I don't know its name. That colored one shaped like a shield.

Students may also elaborate on the meaning or paraphrase the main idea. This is what people do naturally, in their own or another language, when someone misunderstands what has been said. On realizing a misunderstanding has taken place, the speaker tries again. Phrases that might help students elaborate include *I mean*, *In other words*, and *Let me try to explain again*.

Using Dictionaries or Translation Apps

Although teachers may like their students to use strategies other than resorting to a dictionary or translation app, the reality is that technology today makes looking a word up quick and easy. When time and situation allow, a speaker can pull out a cell phone, tap in or say a word, and show it to the other person in less time than it takes to explain. Try looking up a word in one of the popular online learner dictionaries: *Cambridge Learner's Dictionary*, *Longman English Dictionary Online*, or *Merriam-Webster Learner's Dictionary*.

Code-Switching or Word Coinage

Sometimes students will *code-switch*, or use their first language with others who speak the same language, when they do not know a specific vocabulary word. Other times, they will create a new word (*word coinage*) based on their knowledge of their first language and English. Depending on the word that is created, listeners may or may not understand the speaker's meaning. To allow students to experiment with language, teachers can avoid instituting strict English-only policies.

Change the Subject

For language learners, changing the subject is a good strategy when they do not know anything about the topic being discussed. This happens often in L1 conversations. People taking part in a conversation want to talk about something else. Maybe they are bored or do not know anything about the topic, or perhaps they think that everything that can be said has been said. Look at how Speaker C manages to change the topic here:

A. It's not easy learning the piano, is it?

B. No, it's not. But I think some people are better at music than others.

A. Why do you think that is?

B. That's just what I've noticed.

C. Mmm. You might be right. That reminds me of when I was learning to play football . . .

Notice that speaker C, who has been silent so far, introduces a topic that is similar (the topic of learning), yet different (football instead of music). Students can learn the words and phrases that help them steer the talk toward something they know about, such as *By the way*, *That reminds me*, and *Speaking of*.

Planning and Rehearsal

Teachers can help students to plan for intimidating situations. For example, if students express that they have had difficulty communicating at the bank, you can help them to plan and practice what the teller might say and their responses. Then, they can be encouraged to do the same on their own the next time they face an intimidating situation.

REFLECTIVE QUESTIONS

- In addition to the communication strategies listed here, how have you repaired breakdowns in communication?

- Which of the strategies here or the ones you listed above would most help your students handle breakdowns?

Conclusion

Speaking is a process not only of learning forms and stringing them together in conversational contexts but also of conversing politely in the larger context of the real world (sociocultural competence). Moreover, communicating in the real world means learning how to prepare for and deal with communication breakdowns (strategic competence). To assist students in developing these competencies, the following chapters explore how to prepare for speaking classes.

CHAPTER 4

Ways of Teaching Speaking

What do you think should happen during a speaking lesson or course? Take a few moments to write down some ideas.

REFLECTIVE QUESTION

● A typical speaking lesson would involve _____ .

Answers to the Reflective Question may range from "getting students talking as much as possible" to "giving learners some tools of language so that they can speak English." Both views may work, but going too far in either direction can be problematic.

Teaching speaking is not simply a matter of getting students to open their mouths and talk. To develop learners' communicative competence as it relates to speaking, teachers may teach grammar, pronunciation, vocabulary, communication strategies, sociocultural information, or the subskills of speaking or listening.

Teaching speaking, on the other hand, is not primarily a process of conveying "rules" to students. Speaking classrooms often do not prepare learners for actual communication (Hughes, 2010). Knowledge is one thing, applying it is another. The way rules are learned and practiced and the practices themselves are as important, if not more so, than the rules. This chapter looks at ways of teaching that help students use language to communicate in English.

Activities for Conveying Rules

As with other kinds of teaching, two broad options exist for letting students learn the "rules." One is to offer language samples and help them discover the rules, and the other is to start with some direct teaching of guidelines and then show examples. Some ways of using these two options are listed in Table 4.1

Table 4.1. Discovery Learning and Direct Teaching

Content	Discovery	Direct
Communication strategy: keeping a conversation going	Methods are presented in dialogues that the students then analyze.	Ways are listed for students: "Here are X ways to keep a conversation going."
Grammar and sociocultural information: modals for giving advice (could, should, had better, etc.)	Students watch video clips and then, with a partner, decide which modals for giving advice are appropriate in each situation and why. Pairs write rules for using modals.	Modals for giving advice are listed on a continuum from weak to strong and explained with examples. Sociocultural information about when to use which modal is also explained.

Because discovery learning is often done in pairs or groups and increases opportunities for in-class communication, it works well in speaking courses. However, direct teaching can be an efficient way of conveying rules, and even when done in a whole-class setting, it usually involves a large amount of teacher-student interaction. Many teachers weave discovery learning and direct teaching together as they focus on fluency and accuracy.

The first example (fig. 4.1) is a handout for students in a direct instruction lesson on prepositions of time. The teacher introduces the grammar rules and then students practice using the rules.

Direct Instruction: Prepositions of Time

Prepositions are words like *on* and *in* that come before a noun or pronoun to show the noun's or pronoun's relationship to other words in the sentence.

In and On	Example
In + part of day	Veronica eats breakfast **in** the morning.
In + month	Omar goes to Saudi Arabia **in** April.
In + year	I was born **in** 1980.
In + season	Mike buys apples **in** the fall.
On + date	My birthday is **on** April 10, 1990.
On + day	Her appointment is **on** Tuesday.
At + time	My meeting is **at** 3:00.

Complete the following sentences with *in*, *on*, or *at*.

1. I'm going there _____ Monday.
2. The meeting's _____ the 3rd of June.
3. The course starts _____ autumn.
4. She was born _____ 2002.
5. It happened _____ a Wednesday.
6. I lost my purse _____ the winter.
7. We will begin _____ noon.
8. My birthday is _____ Valentine's Day.
9. I will go to school _____ August 15.
10. The class is _____ Mondays.

Figure 4.1. Direct Instruction Student Handout

The second example (fig. 4.2) is a handout given to students in a discovery-learning lesson on the same topic, prepositions of time. The teacher helps students to notice the rules as they read a paragraph multiple times with different purposes.

Discovery Learning: Prepositions of Time

Read the paragraph. During the first reading, underline all of the words related to time. During the second reading, circle the words that come before the time words/phrases. The first one has been done for you.

My name is Isabella. I was born (on) August 8 in San Pedro Sula, Honduras. I don't tell everyone when, but I will tell you. I was born in 1982. I live in Boston. In summer, we try to go to the beach. In winter, I like to stay home, because it is too cold here. You should visit Boston in October, because the trees here are so pretty! I am a student in English classes now. I have class in the morning and in the evening. At noon, I like to eat lunch, and I take a nap at 1:00 p.m. We only have class on Monday, Tuesday, and Wednesday. On Thursday and Friday, I work at my uncle's store. I like to study and spend time with family on Saturday and Sunday.

What words come before the following?

_____ Time (2:00)   _____ Month (April)

_____ Part of the day (the night)   _____ Season (summer)

_____ Day (Monday)   _____ Year (1990)

_____ Date (June 1)

Answer the following questions with full sentences.

1. When were you born? _____

2. What days do you go to school? _____

3. What time does school start? _____

4. What year was your daughter born? _____

5. When do you like to eat ice cream? (season) _____

6. What month do you like to drink tea or coffee in? _____

7. When is your favorite time of day? _____

8. What time does class start? _____

Figure 4.2. Discovery Learning Student Handout

Activities for Practicing

Richards (2006) summarizes ways of categorizing activities, including mechanical, meaningful, and communicative activities. To understand the differences between these types of activities, picture them on a continuum ranging from controlled, traditional drills to free practice, where real communication occurs. Figure 4.3 includes some of the characteristics that might be found on this spectrum.

Because the goal of teaching speaking is to develop students' ability to speak in English, getting to and spending adequate time at the communicative end of the continuum is vital. Depending on students' level, though, they may not be capable of completing a communicative activity without first practicing at the mechanical or meaningful stage.

Types of Activities

When teaching speaking, what types of activities should teachers use? What should they do for students? Take a few moments to list some ideas in the Reflective Question.

REFLECTIVE QUESTION

- Speaking activities should _____.

mechanical	meaningful	communicative
not necessarily contextualized	contextualized	meaningful, real world contexts
for the purpose of learning language	for the purpose of using language in order to deepen understanding	for the purpose of using language to communicate
focused on accuracy	focused on accuracy leading toward fluency	focused on fluency
not necessarily interactive	interaction about language or with language in controlled situations	interaction and negotiation with language

Figure 4.3. The Activities Continuum

Deciding what activities to use can be challenging. Sometimes the countless activities to choose from can be overwhelming, and sometimes a lack of resources is the challenge. The following list of characteristics of speaking activities illustrated with examples may help. Then, the next section will discuss how to put the activities together into lessons.

Imitating Real-World Communication

The goal of teaching speaking is to enable students to speak English in real situations. In class, teachers may be working their way toward this as they facilitate communicative practice, but even activities in the middle and toward the left side of the continuum can imitate real-world communication (see Figure 4.4). Notice how the example activity "Saying Good-bye" does this while flowing from mechanical and meaningful to communicative.

Role-playing, often used to practice appropriate and polite ways of performing speech acts, lends itself well to real-world communication. In fact, it may be so real that it elicits actual emotion. For instance, when a group of students was asked to do a practice like "Saying Good-bye," their communication was so real that Role-Play 2 brought tears to their eyes. Activities like this may also encourage learners to take communication outside the classroom and into the real world.

REFLECTIVE QUESTIONS

- Role-playing can be easily changed so that it imitates the specific world of students. Would the "Saying Good-bye" activity work with your students? If not, how could you change it to make it work?

Saying Good-bye

Introduction

Think about the words for saying good-bye and the politeness rules we've talked about. Work with a partner and decide how you would say good-bye and respond in these two situations. Be prepared to explain.

- It's the end of class on Friday afternoon. Classmates are saying good-bye to each other.
- Someone got a new job, and it's his or her last day at the old job.

Role-Play 1

Role play the following situations with your partner. Try to use the words and follow the politeness rules we talked about.

Person A	Person B
1. At the end of class, say good-bye to your friend who you'll see tomorrow.	Respond to your friend.
2. Respond to your friend as s/he says good-bye before going home for a few months.	You're returning to your hometown for a few months. Say good-bye to your friend.
3. You're a store manager who is being moved to a new store. Your employee is saying good-bye. Respond to her/his words.	Your manager is moving to a new store. He or she has helped you a lot. Say good-bye.
4. The school is on holiday next week. Say good-bye to your student.	Respond to your teacher.

Role-Play 2

Pretend that today is the last day of class. You probably won't see many of your classmates or teacher again. Stand up, walk around the room, and say good-bye.

Adapted from Dirksen and Smith (2002)

Figure 4.4. Example Activity

Calling for Communication

One problem with speaking activities is that they sometimes ask students to do something in pairs that could just as easily be done alone. Activities that, instead, create or make use of a gap in knowledge necessitate communication. This type of task cannot be completed unless two or more students use their combined knowledge.

Information-gap activities are specifically designed to require genuine communication (Doughty & Pica, 1986). Because one person has information the other needs, students are motivated to talk with each other. In a classic information-gap activity, one student describes a picture while another draws it without looking at the original. One way this could be used in a progression of activities is in a lesson focused on travel, potentially with some attention given to article usage. As part of the lesson, pairs take turns describing two different pictures. The partner listens and draws. Pairs then use the drawings to design the lesson's culminating project: brochures advertising a local tourist attraction.

Interviews and *opinion-gap activities* motivate communication because students gather previously unknown information from their classmates.

Information Gap Activity: Who Are My Classmates? Fill in the boxes below with information after interviewing two classmates. Ask the questions in the boxes, and respond with complete sentences.			
Name What is your name?	**Hometown** Where are you from?	**Family** How many people are in your family? Who are they?	**Occupation** What is your job?

The example activity "Who Are My Classmates?" is an interview that collects factual information. If we add a question, *What do you like about learning English?*, it also becomes an opinion-gap activity. Because it collects unknown information (and possibly opinions), it motivates communication.

Getting Lost in Communication

One way to prepare students for real-world communication is to get them lost in communication and unaware of the classroom. Opinion-gap activities or discussions can facilitate this.

One key to a communicative discussion is asking good questions that elicit opinions and feelings. The point is to immerse students in the activity, which is what happened with some adult Chinese students who were asked to come to a group consensus about this question: who is the most influential person in Chinese history? The discussion was heated but amiable.

Another key is for teachers to give students control of the discussion. One teacher did this in a whole-class setting by choosing not to respond to students' contributions. His silence opened the door for learners to reply to each other and take ownership of the discussion. If teachers frequently interrupt with corrections or elaborate on learners' contributions, it may be difficult for them to get lost in communication.

Projects can also get students lost in communication. These are often used as culminating activities and ask students to take everything learned in a unit (or over a series of lessons) and put it together to make something new. The group of first-year university students who completed the example activity "Creating a Family Tree" were practicing family relationship vocabulary, describing people, and pronouncing /ð/ (pronounced as the *th* sound in *the* or *mother*).

Developing Accuracy that Leads to Fluency

As mentioned earlier, teaching speaking involves focusing on both accuracy and fluency. Accuracy is important and vital for fluency to occur, but getting stuck in the accuracy (or mechanical) stage is all too easy. One remedy may be to move form-focused activities, even mechanical practices when possible, toward real-world communication. Even drills are more meaningful, not to mention interesting, when teachers can add a real-world context, preferably the context of the lesson, and make drills or practices interactive. Problem-solving activities do this. Although they could be done individually, the challenge of figuring out the answers motivates interaction because students intuitively know that two heads are better than one. For example, while learning family relationship vocabulary, the students could answer tricky questions like "Who is the mother of my niece's mother?"

Creating a Family Tree

Part 1: Students work in groups of four. Each group member is assigned to play the role of one of these family members: grandfather or grandmother, second cousin, great-niece or great-nephew, or brother-in-law or sister-in-law. Then, groups create a family tree on large paper using pictures from magazines to represent themselves and different family members.

Part 2: Groups post family trees around the classroom. Two family members stay to answer questions; two rotate around the room looking at other family trees. Then, presenters switch with observers for a second round of rotating. Students vote on their favorite poster.

Part 3: Students bring photos of their actual families to introduce in small groups during the next class.

Games are often nothing more than pattern drills in interesting contexts that require interaction. Take, for example, a guessing game in a lesson in the context of heroes. Each group of four has a set of cards displaying the names of well-known heroes. One student draws a card and gives clues following this sentence pattern using the past perfect:

> By the time s/he _____ (became famous/won the Nobel Prize/retired/
> died) ____, s/he had _____.

The student who guesses correctly gets to keep the card, and the student with the most cards wins.

Lesson Planning

Putting activities together into a workable lesson plan can be tricky. Not all students are the same, so their starting and ending points may differ. Some will need to start with mechanical and meaningful activities, and others will be able to communicate and fine-tune the mechanics as they go. Some ideas follow; also see the appendix for a sample lesson plan.

Start With the Big Picture

First, think about learners' needs, which are the foundation for curriculum development (Richards, 2017). What is your class preparing them for? What do they need for future classes? How do or will they use English outside of class? Then, think about the end result, and decide how to get there. Where should students be by the end of your course? What real-world communication should they be able to participate in by the end of the term? Answering these questions will give you a big-picture view of where you are headed and help you develop goals or outcomes for a course.

Consider the Smaller Picture

Once the big picture is in place, you can start focusing on some of the details. What are the smaller steps, or the weekly or daily lessons, that will lead to the end goals? Where should students be, or what real-world communication should they be able to participate in by the end of a lesson (or unit)? What do they need to get there? It might help to write out some ideas (objectives) before you try to put together a lesson.

Put the Pieces Together

How you put each lesson plan together depends on where your students are and where they need to be. If they seem to need some exposure to the rules of language, you may want to design lessons that flow from the mechanical end of the continuum to the communicative. For example, when teaching a speech act, you could begin with some discussion of the rules (whether by discovery learning or direct teaching). Then, in the first practice activity, students may be repeating the conversation of others. As the activities progress, the words become more their own. Role-play, where they are given some support but the general flow of the conversation is set out, is a good halfway point. Finally, they gain the confidence and ability to perform the speech act in real-world situations using their own words. Other students may have had a good deal of exposure to rules but few chances to apply them. If you think your students need a review of the rules, then you could try a discovery-learning activity. What learners need most, though, is practice.

Some research (e.g., Long, 1983; Gass, 1997) shows that speaking ability develops through interaction or, more specifically, negotiation (the back-and-forth communication between speakers to convey meaning). If this type of learning is what your students seem to need, then your lessons will be made up of a series of communicative tasks that provide practice in one of the situations you have identified in their target context. As students try to convey meaning in each practice, they may learn from each other: for example, a new word, a structure, or even how to pronounce something. If they struggle in a particular area, you can prepare an accuracy-focused practice for them before moving on to the next practice. (This type of lesson follows the focus on form vs. focus on forms pattern mentioned in chapter 2.)

REFLECTIVE QUESTIONS

- Choose one of the example activities in this chapter. Think about the following questions:
    - Would it work with your students? Why? How could you adapt it?
    - What type of lesson would you use it in?
    - Where and how would it fit into a lesson?

Conclusion

Organizing lesson plans involves many choices. Once teachers understand their students' needs, they can find activities that provide the support or scaffolding required for students to get lost in communication, and they can move from providing more support to allowing students to communicate more freely inside or outside the classroom.

CHAPTER 5

Ways of Using Speaking to Teach

In end-of-semester feedback in a TESOL methods course in China, students mentioned that the teacher's style encouraged them to develop oral proficiency. The teacher used a discussion-based approach for this graduate-level course and incorporated discovery learning activities. Drawing on their background knowledge, students worked together, with varying degrees of teacher participation, to figure out principles and techniques. In the process, the students practiced speaking, a vital skill for preservice English teachers.

Situations similar to the one described here are common, especially in EFL settings, where English is not widely spoken outside of the classroom. Students need to develop oral proficiency, but the course focuses on content like methods, culture, literature, linguistics, and oral interpretation. Even oral courses involve some content, including culture, discourse, and language "rules," and teachers would like to increase opportunities for in-class communication but are not sure how. One way to solve these problems is to use speaking to teach. The next few sections will give you some ideas about how to do this.

Different Views of Using Speaking to Teach

Instead of direct teaching, this chapter encourages you to try some discovery learning. Worked into the following text are questions, tasks, and Reflective Questions that encourage you to discover how to use speaking to teach. At the same time, we also directly present theories and techniques. In keeping with the spirit of the discussion, you could collaborate with a speaking partner as you work through the next few paragraphs. Alternatively, you can reflect individually as you read.

Social Constructivism

One theory that comes into play when using speaking to teach is social constructivism. Before directly explaining it, however, and contrasting it with a different approach—transmission—see what you can puzzle out.

The phrase "using speaking to teach" is in some ways self-explanatory. When you look at the sentences below, which ones seem to describe how to use speaking to teach?

A. Lessons are designed around what the teacher says. Students mostly listen.

B. Students come up with their own understandings of what is being learned by interacting with and learning from each other.

C. The teacher is the expert filling up students with knowledge.

D. The teacher (through activities) draws on students' background knowledge and ideas, which they use to figure out correct answers.

E. Lessons are designed around what students do. The teacher mostly facilitates.

F. The teacher directly tells students the right answers.

Now, consider these two contrasting models of teaching—constructivism (B, D, E) and transmission (A, C, F). When you look at the words themselves, what do you see that tells you what they mean? You can also use the preceding sentences to find answers to the following questions.

Transmission	Constructivism
Who transmits?	Who constructs?
What do they transmit?	What do they construct?
To whom?	How?

REFLECTIVE QUESTION

● How do your answers compare to our direct explanation below?

Social constructivism is an education theory that has been applied to language teaching. It "champion[s] social interaction, discovery learning, and the active role of the learner as necessary for effective learning" (Brown, 2014, p. 13). In contrast to transmission or direct teaching, lessons are designed around what students say and do. Learners build understandings of knowledge in cooperation with others, including classmates, teachers, and parents, instead of receiving what teachers transmit to them.

Based on your understandings, combined with your teaching and learning experiences, you may have a picture in your mind of what these two theories (transmission and constructivism) encompass. If you were to put that picture on paper, what would it look like? Take a few minutes to draft diagrams of the two theories on paper or using your computer. In the Reflective Questions, compare your diagrams to ours.

REFLECTIVE QUESTIONS

● How do your two diagrams compare to ours? What do the details in the constructivist diagram tell you?

● How does the constructivist diagram seem to fit (or not fit) with what happened in the TESOL methods course described at the beginning of this chapter?

● Where and how does oral proficiency develop in the constructivist diagram?

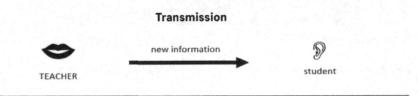

Transmission

new information

TEACHER   student

Figure 5.1. Transmission Diagram

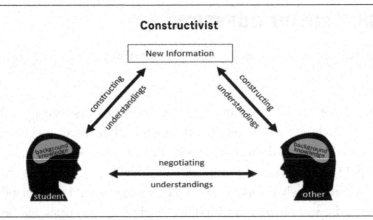

Constructivist

New Information

constructing
understandings

constructing
understandings

background knowledge

background knowledge

negotiating

understandings

student   other

Figure 5.2 Constructivist Diagram

Interaction Hypothesis

The students who felt that their oral skills improved in their TESOL methods course were experiencing interaction hypothesis in action. Interaction
hypothesis says that language learning occurs in the context of communication as learners interact or negotiate with each other, their teacher, or
someone else. In this way, "conversation is not only a medium of practice; it
is also the means by which learning takes place" (Gass 1997, p. 104). When
using speaking to teach, that is exactly what happens. Learners communicate
with each other to acquire content, and, in the process, their speaking (and
other language) skills may develop.

REFLECTIVE QUESTION

- What types of activities may best encourage interaction that
  leads to improved oral proficiency?

Communicative Language Teaching and Task-Based Language Teaching

As you may have noted during the Reflective Question, not just any type of interaction or activity will lead to language development. In fact, you may have used words similar to those found in descriptions of CLT and task-based language teaching (TBLT). In simple terms, CLT underscores the use of language (communication) to learn language, in other words, using speaking to teach. In addition, it specifies that this type of communication should be meaningful and authentic, encourage fluency and accuracy, while emphasizing all aspects of communicative competence (Brown & Lee, 2015).

TBLT says that the communicative learning process occurs in the classroom in the context of meaningful, real-world tasks that are set up as problems to be solved (Brown, 2014). When using speaking to teach, these meaningful tasks give learners an opportunity to interact authentically as they solve problems (like those you are solving as you work through this chapter) related to the content being taught.

Cooperative Learning

Cooperative learning is an idea from the field of education that fits well in the language classroom, especially when using speaking to teach. Your answers to some of the last Reflective Questions may have included some of its defining characteristics. Pairs or groups of students work together like teams on which every member actively works toward a common goal and at the same time builds relationships within their classroom community.

REFLECTIVE QUESTIONS

Following are two samples that demonstrate the constructivist model. Consider these questions as you study them:

- What do you imagine the interaction and cooperation between students might look like?

- In what ways are students asked to construct understandings of information in each?

- What problems are students asked to solve?

- What seems reversed (from a traditional transmission style) in the two samples?

continued on next page

SAMPLE 1: FAMILY SNOWBALL

Objective: By the end of this activity, students will be able to identify some family relationship terms.

Procedures:

1. The teacher projects her photo family tree on the screen.
2. Pairs use words from the chart to identify and describe their teacher's family members. When they use a word or phrase, they put a ✔ next to it. (For example, students may say sentences like the following: *Sue is her mom. David is her dad. She has 3 sisters. Her older sister has 4 children. These are her nieces and nephews.*)
3. Pairs first get together with another pair (forming groups of 4), and then in a third round, each group of 4 gets together with another group of 4 (forming groups of 8). Each round, groups compare words/phrases they have put a ✔ next to and teach each other. They continue to identify and describe the teacher's family members and put a ✔ next to words/phrases they use.
4. The class works together to identify and describe family members. If necessary, they refer to an L1-English dictionary. The teacher may provide some feedback or guidance where needed.

mother/mom	wife	grandmother/ma	great grandmother/ma
father/dad	husband	grandfather/pa	great grandfather/pa
sister	daughter	granddaughter	great granddaughter
brother	son	grandson	great grandson
aunt		great aunt	in-law
uncle		great uncle	older/oldest
niece		great niece	younger/youngest
nephew		great nephew	
cousin			

SAMPLE 2: ORAL INTERPRETATION ANALYSIS

Objective: By the end of this activity, students will be able to identify and describe characteristics of a skillful interpretation and interpreting techniques.

Procedures

1. Before Class: The teacher posted a video clip of a professional interpretation to the course website. The students watched the clip and identified interpreting techniques from a list provided by the teacher.
2. In-Class Group Work: In groups of 3-4, the students re-watch portions of the interpretation and discuss this question: *Based on what you see in the video, what do you think makes an interpretation skillful?* Groups take notes and prepare to share their ideas with the whole class.
3. Follow up Discussion: The teacher facilitates a follow up discussion in which ideas are elicited from groups, refined if necessary, and listed on the board in a T-chart like the following. The teacher highlights techniques they have already learned and encourages students to add new ones.

what TO DO when interpreting	what TO AVOID when interpreting

Flipped Learning

When you answered the last Reflective Questions, you may have noted a reversal in roles. It seems that the students become the teacher. Also, in Sample 2, transmission seems to happen at home and practice in class rather than vice versa. These reversals, especially the second, characterize another view of using speaking to teach—flipped learning.

Imagine two different sides of a coin. Transmission is on one side, activities or practice on the other. In a traditional classroom, transmission happens in class; if practice happens, it occurs after class in the homework assignment. In a flipped classroom, the coin is reversed, and transmission happens first as a preclass homework assignment. For example, the students read a text and complete some comprehension exercises, or they listen to a recorded lecture the teacher gives. Then, in class they engage in practice activities that help them process content at a deeper level. When using speaking to teach, "content-rich subjects . . . can be flipped so that students get 'up to speed' with the content outside the classroom and the teacher can then concentrate on having the students talk about the content when the class comes together in school" (Harmer, 2015, p. 206).

Reflecting on the Two Models

REFLECTIVE QUESTIONS

Reflect on how you have learned while working through this chapter. We were trying to give you a taste of the constructivist model (and, if you were working with a partner, of using speaking to teach).

- If you were a student, how would this approach to learning make you feel? Why?

- How might your feelings differ were your teacher to follow the transmission model and teach you directly?

While answering the Reflective Questions, you may have been thinking that regardless of your feelings, using a constructivist approach is difficult in your context. It can be challenging to use constructivist approaches where transmission has a rich history. To illustrate this, a teacher from a traditional context observed one of us using a jigsaw activity. The 24 students started in groups of four, and each group became experts in one of three sets of material (A, B, and C). Then, like a jigsaw puzzle, students formed new groups of three with one A, one B, and one C in each. In their new groups, each student took turns teaching their two new group members the materials they prepared in the previous group until all three sections were learned. Although the observer tried to be diplomatic, she shook her head and reported that she could never teach this way because it wasn't teaching. When students are tasked with the creating understandings of knowledge, much of the "teaching" looks different. It happens in the preparation of materials, the organization of learning experiences, and the careful guidance during class time, but accepting this approach can be difficult for those who are unaccustomed to it.

REFLECTIVE QUESTIONS

Take a few minutes to evaluate your own teaching.

- Where does it fall between transmission and the constructivist approach?

- How would you assess your approach to teaching? Reflect on the following questions as you assess:
    - Which model would your students like more?
    - Which one is better for them? Which one most meets their speaking needs, and how?
    - What are some changes, if any, you'd like to make to your teaching based on your assessment?

Suggestions for Using Speaking to Teach

The preceding paragraphs led you to contrast direct ways of teaching with constructivist approaches and presented a model of how to use speaking to teach. The following advice shows how this approach may play out in the classroom.

Encouraging Cooperation

To encourage cooperative learning and ensure that every team member participates, keep groups small, 2–4 members each. Some teachers have found learning teams helpful. These set groups can be used for a month, a semester, or even throughout an entire program, and, while they may not be used for every activity, they work well for larger and end-of-unit, culminating projects.

Activating Meaningful Communication

To make interaction purposeful, give pairs or groups clearly defined, common goals to work toward. Also, ask them to produce something that demonstrates how well they have reached the stated goals. This could be a handout they fill out, or, depending on where you are in the content-learning process, it could be an illustration, chart, poster, podcast, or action plan.

Setting up Problem-Based Learning

Design the in-class learning of content as a series of problems to be solved. These problems may flow from lower-order thinking skills (LOTS)—remembering, understanding, applying—to higher-order thinking skills (HOTS)—analyzing, evaluating, creating. For example, they may start by asking students to identify or interpret concepts; then learners organize information or draw principles from examples; and, finally, they evaluate ideas or engage in self-assessment before putting what they learned into practice in the real world.

Flipping the Classroom

On occasions when learners need a base of knowledge to complete in-class tasks, flip the classroom and assign homework for that purpose. Consider, however, what students may need to acquire that base. Is, for example, reading or listening to a lecture enough, or do they also need to complete a few LOTS tasks to give them a firmer foundation for in-class problem-solving?

Empowering Learners by Using Speaking to Teach

You were asked to consider how you and your students may feel about constructivist approaches. Perhaps the word *empowered* came to mind. An experienced teacher reflected on an old saying and expanded it this way (the underlined portion is her addition): *Tell me, and I forget. Show me, and I remember. Involve me, and I understand. Engage me, and I create. Empower me, and I am a master.*

REFLECTIVE QUESTION

- How does this teacher's expansion on an old saying inspire you to try using speaking to teach?

CHAPTER 6

Challenges of Teaching Speaking Communicatively

Today, teachers face a variety of challenges and environmental constraints depending on where they teach. Some have well-equipped classrooms with rich English resources outside of the classroom. Others are limited by a lack of resources or by rules and regulations.

REFLECTIVE QUESTIONS

- What is the biggest challenge you face in teaching speaking?
- Who or what can help you to overcome this challenge?

One of the biggest challenges teachers around the world face comes when they try to apply CLT in a traditional setting. When teachers from traditional classrooms attend workshops on using communicative activities, they often raise objections. Here are some responses to these concerns, based on the experiences of teachers in many different countries.

Some Common Challenges

Noise Levels

When classes are large and teachers in adjoining rooms expect silence, the level of noise can be a valid concern. What can a teacher do?

- Discuss the problem with a supervisor. Colleagues need to understand that noise comes from language classrooms, and especially speaking classrooms, some of the time.

- Invite students to whisper for some activities.

- Warn the teacher next door that a few minutes into the lesson there will be talking, but only for a few moments.

Interestingly, when the loud noise comes from entire classes chorusing the same thing, it is often considered normal. Thus, our explanations may need to address both the decibels and the uncontrolled nature of the talking.

Movement Restrictions or Fixed Furniture

Some teachers are unable to move the desks in their classrooms or cannot create groups of students or monitor group work because of the configuration of the furniture.

- Try rotating the seating plan so a different group of students sits at the front each week.

- Have a student take on the role of recorder to keep a record of what occurred in the group. You could collect these papers.

- Make the best use of the classroom space possible. For example, in large classrooms where not all desks are used, have students sit near the aisles rather than filling the first few rows.

- Not all communicative activities involve moving around the room. Agile students can easily twist around in their seats to do pair and group work.

- Have students move to an open space at the front or the side of the classroom and form two "talk lines" or "talk circles." One row can move so that they are talking to a new student every few minutes.

- Some schools will allow teachers to send students into the corridors or even outside for a few moments.

Students Speaking L1 at Inappropriate Times

Some students make use of their L1 during communicative activities.

- Explain to students that it is fine to use their L1 to sort out the "rules" of the activity, especially in beginner classes, or to negotiate meaning when other efforts have failed.

- Use positive reinforcement. While walking round the room, note groups who are using English and reward them in some way at the end of class.

- Negotiate how L1 will be used in the classroom on the first day of class, creating a list of guidelines. This allows students to feel their L1 is being respected and that they have some control in the classroom.

- Consider embracing L1 as a linguistic resource. Translanguaging moves beyond viewing the use of all possible languages as code-switching to viewing a learner's many languages as part of his or her "linguistic repertoire" (Otheguy, Garcia, & Reid, 2015).

Limited Time

Some teachers fear not finishing the chapter if they stop and allow students to speak. In some schools, teachers must keep pace with other classes. Remember that using the new language is not an optional extra, it is the goal of a language class.

- Link activities to the textbook so that the chapter is being finished as the lesson proceeds.

- Use speaking to teach (see chapter 5). Group and pair work are often efficient ways to cover needed content and allow for authentic interaction.

- Consider "flipping" the classroom (see chapter 5) and assigning some of the content as preclass work or as homework.

Unengaged Students

Some students are reserved or do not want to lose face, so they do not feel comfortable speaking in groups. Others may wish to talk, but strong class-mates take most of the discussion time. Some students may simply feel they have nothing to share. Other students may think that speaking English is not worthwhile or that practice activities are just games and not real learning.

- Use Think-Pair-Share or Think-Write-Pair-Share activities. In both cases, allowing students time to think, possibly also to write, and then practice in pairs may build their confidence before they are asked to speak in larger groups.

- Give each member of the group a role, or try dividing questions and assigning them to group members. Some possible roles include facilitator, recorder, checker, reporter, timekeeper, devil's advocate (who challenges ideas), and language monitor.

- Consider a participation system in groups, where each learner is given a set number of tokens or other items like popsicle sticks he or she places in the middle of the desk after speaking.

- Create tasks that require each participant to contribute, such as the information gap and interview activities described in chapter 4.

- Use a set up like numbered heads together, where each student in each group has a number (13 or–4, for example, depending on group size), and then during whole-class follow-up, call on group members to share by number: "All the 2s, please stand up. Who would like to tell us what your group decided?"

- Design activities that relate to students' lives, are pleasurable, and are within their ability level.

- Explore the reason for each activity and what achieving its outcomes would look like.

- Work toward a greater, change-the-world-style purpose (Pink, 2009).

REFLECTIVE QUESTIONS

- What are some steps you could take to make learning more pleasurable for your students?

- What speaking activities might inspire them to devise and potentially act on solutions to local or world problems?

Lack of Confidence in English

Sometimes teachers lack confidence in their own oral English skills.

- Teachers who teach in a traditional way spend hours of effort preparing to explain the majority of the information in the text. If they put the same preparation into communicative lessons, they may find their confidence level growing.

- Some teachers worry about being prepared for the unexpected. In communicative activities and lessons, teachers do not have complete control over what happens. They can and should put some limits on the direction of the class, though. They can also make use of replies such as, "That's a good question, but let's talk about it next week when we have more time." Another approach is to look for the answer together by saying something like, "I want you to learn to use your resources to answer language questions. Let's look up the information together, so that you'll be able to do it in the future."

- Teachers can see the challenge of preparing to speak in communicative lessons as good motivation to be lifelong language learners.

Other Personal or Philosophical Barriers

When teachers were asked to consider reasons for their reluctance to use CLT activities in their classrooms, some expressed confusion about where to begin planning. Others felt overwhelmed by managing activities in large classes, especially with students lacking motivation or confidence. Some were concerned about not meeting the expectations of students or a supervisor who had told them to talk more in class. Still others were struggling to see the value of practice in their exam-based system.

Later, one of the teachers described the "revolution" her teaching underwent. When she invited a guest to teach her 50 students communicatively using her textbook, she finally started to grasp how to use activities. Two others experienced a sort of epiphany when a workshop inspired them to experiment with communicative activities, and they saw desired results. In one case, students finally understood a grammar structure the teacher had been trying—unsuccessfully—to get across. In the other, the teacher reached the positive and engaging atmosphere he had been seeking.

Conclusion

Finally, remember that teachers have been using communicative language activities in classrooms for more than four decades, even in classrooms with large numbers, fixed furniture, and colleagues who raise objections. There are ways around the problems. As teachers move forward and embrace communication in the English language classroom, they can provide meaningful practice for their students and help them to feel more confident and successful in their speaking.

CHAPTER 7

Assessing Progress in Speaking

This chapter explores ways to extend or enhance learning. One way this happens is through outside-of-class assignments. The chapter also discusses how to encourage and measure learning through ongoing and final assessments.

Outside-of-Class Assignments

When the topic of outside-of-class assignments comes up, teachers may ask two questions: what type should be given, and how often? First, it may be helpful to look at some purposes of outside work. Three are listed here.

1. *Preview:* Some assignments prepare for the next class. Students might complete textbook exercises that hone the language tools needed to participate in practice activities. They might find materials, pictures of their family or hometown, for example, and prepare to talk about them. They could also listen to a report or read an article to prepare for a discussion or debate. In a flipped learning model, this preclass work becomes the input that students will use in the classroom.

2. *Reinforcement:* Many between-class tasks ask students to use what they learned in a new way or to transfer a knowledge or skill from one situation to another. Often these assignments take students one step closer to real-world communication as they apply them to their lives or use them in actual communication outside the classroom.

3. *Assessment:* Out-of-class work often acts as an assessment tool for teachers. Whether students complete something in writing, report orally, or use their prepared work in a class activity, teachers have a chance to see whether or not their course and lesson objectives are being met.

Outside-of-class work can be a single task that relates to a particular lesson or a project connected to a unit or series of units. For example, in an advertising unit, students might create and perform a commercial advertising their oral English course. It may also involve assignments that students complete at regular intervals throughout a course: an oral practice log or journal. Outside-of-class work can be completed individually or in pairs or groups. Whatever the form, teachers may need to figure out a balance between what students need and what is realistic (for students to complete and for teachers to grade).

Some outside-of-class tasks you might use are listed here.

- Group presentations: In a unit on cross-cultural communication, ask groups to prepare presentations on cultural norms.

- Interviews or surveys: In a unit on values, ask students to prepare a survey to research some aspect of the topic (how culture influences values, perhaps). They could then interview their classmates or another group outside of class.

- Ongoing oral activities: At the beginning of the semester, provide a list of level-appropriate activities that require students to speak English. They choose a set number to complete individually or in a group before the end of the semester.

- English corners or clubs: These might be held once a week in an informal setting, and students are required to attend a certain number of times in a semester.
  - Recorded speech: Students can record responses to prompts or classmates on a cell phone. To allow students to record group conversations and to encourage speaking outside of class, they can upload a recording or write a summary.

Ongoing and Final Assessment

Although many options are available for assessing speaking, using actual speaking tasks indicates to students that oral communication is valuable. Large classes may sometimes make this seem impossible, but creative formats such as group exams or uploading speech samples to a learning management system can be used. It is important not to lose sight of the goals for your course when you are creating speaking assessments. A close relationship should exist between what you planned for students to learn and how or what you evaluate.

Regardless of how you evaluate speaking, using a rubric with explicit scoring criteria for any oral task is important (see the sample rubric that follows). This will help students to see where improvement is needed and that the evaluation is not arbitrary. It also creates clear criteria for you and any other potential evaluators. Nation (2011) suggests these categories be included in a speaking rubric: fluency, intelligibility, grammatical accuracy, vocabulary, and overall score. Consider which areas most accurately reflect your course goals.

Another approach is to have students self-assess. For example, students could record themselves completing a group speaking task and then use a simplified version of the sample rubric to assess themselves. They could also self-assess class participation in a log that utilizes a scale from 1 (little-to-no participation) to 4 (fully engaged) and then note what influenced their participation. Before class, they could choose a strategy they would like to work on. Then, at the end of class, they assess how successfully they incorporated it.

Sample Rubric

This rubric is used for a group speaking exam.

	Excellent	Proficient	Needs Improvement
Fluency	Student facilitated the progression of the conversation. When potential for communication breakdown occurred, the student assisted with flow.	Student actively participated in the conversation, both providing content and eliciting ideas from others.	Conversation stalled or included pauses or false starts, or the student underparticipated in a way that did not allow for a natural conversation to occur.
Intelligibility	Pronunciation did not inhibit understanding, and intonation and stress were used to enhance meaning. Phonemes focused on in class were clearly articulated (i.e., /y/, /j/, /b/, /v/, /p/, /t/, /k/).	Pronunciation issues influenced intelligibility at times (2–5 times). Most phonemes focused on in class were clearly articulated (i.e., /y/, /j/, /b/, /v/, /p/, /t/, /k/).	Speech was difficult to understand throughout the conversation (5+ times) and/or the phonemes focused on were not clearly articulated (i.e., /y/, /j/, /b/, /v/, /p/, /t/, /k/).
Grammar	Grammar was generally accurate. Structures focused on in class were accurate (i.e., yes/no questions, possessives, prepositions, simple present and past, time clauses, modals).	A few minor grammar errors noted, but communication did not break down. Structures focused on in class were mostly accurate (i.e., yes/no questions, possessives, prepositions, simple present and past, time clauses, modals).	Significant grammar errors led to communication issues. Structures focused on in class were not accurate (i.e., yes/no questions, possessives, prepositions, simple present and past, time clauses, modals).
Vocabulary	At least 10 vocabulary words covered in class were accurately incorporated (i.e., descriptive adjectives, time phrases, food words, daily routines).	At least 5 vocabulary words covered in class were accurately incorporated (i.e., descriptive adjectives, time phrases, food words, daily routines).	Four or fewer studied vocabulary words were included. Communication was hampered due to lack of vocabulary.

Consider guidelines that help to establish levels when your students begin and end their speaking course. See the American Council on the Teaching of Foreign Languages (ACTFL) speaking guidelines (https://www.actfl.org/publications/guidelines-and-manuals/actfl-proficiency-guidelines-2012/english/speaking) or the Common European Framework (https://www.coe.int/en/web/common-european-framework-reference-languages/level-descriptions) as examples.

Some examples of ways to organize quizzes or exams are included here. For students at a lower level, choose those toward the top of the list. Teachers working with a large class could utilize pair or group activities.

- *Dialogues:* Memorized or prepared dialogues allow beginning students to demonstrate their speaking ability without the task being too overwhelming. Repeating dialogues in multiple lessons provides practice with commonly used expressions or multiword chunks of speech that help to build fluency (Hinkel, 2019).

- *Look at a picture; tell a story:* Prepare a number of pictures (or pictures series), and ask students to tell a story. This can be recorded (in a language lab if one is available), which allows larger classes to demonstrate oral skills without the teacher being present with each student during the exam time.

- *Role-playing:* Create scenarios for students based on the content of your course. Give students a fixed period to prepare for role-playing before they perform for you.

- *Presentations:* In an academic setting, students may need to develop presentation skills for future courses. Ask students to present in front of the whole class with visual aids and other linguistic features that are typical in academic presentations (e.g., academic discourse markers).

- *Group discussions:* Prepare discussion questions to be answered after the completion of an in-class or take-home activity such as an interview, a reading, or other tasks, and then ask students to carry on a discussion while you observe. This allows you to evaluate the various aspects of communicative competence covered previously.

- *Recorded projects:* Give students specific criteria to upload a recording of an individual or group movie, documentary, news presentation, or sample teaching as a final project.

- *Interviews:* Interviews allow for individual interaction between teacher and student. They work well for both pretests and posttests but are time consuming for large classes. Before the interviews, try to prepare a number of open-ended questions with some variety but a similar difficulty level. Consider beginning and ending with easy questions or small talk to help students feel relaxed and successful. If time allows, interviews may be recorded to review if there are any questions regarding scoring.

If the culture of the school or country does not allow solely oral final exams, you may consider adding a written component that includes sections on vocabulary, writing or completing dialogues, or politeness.

REFLECTIVE QUESTION

- **Which of the suggestions here would work best in your setting?**

Conclusion

Regardless of your setting, it is important for students, teachers, and administrators to see progress. Students may feel that they are not advancing because there are no set standards. Opportunities to monitor and demonstrate learning benefit everyone involved.

References

Alsagoff, L., McKay, S. L., Hu, G., & Renandya, W. A. (Eds.). (2012). *Principles and practices for teaching English as an international language.* New York, NY: Routledge.

Arevart, S., & Nation, I. S. P. (1991) Fluency improvement in a second language. *RELC Journal, 22*(1), 84–94.

Bohlke, D. (2014). Fluency-oriented second language teaching. In M. Celce-Murcia, D. M. Brinton, & M. A. Snow (Eds.), *Teaching English as a second or foreign language* (4th ed., pp. 121–135). Boston, MA: National Geographic Learning, Heinle-Cengage Learning.

Brown, H. D. (2014). *Principles of language learning and teaching: A course in second language acquisition* (6th ed.). White Plains, NY: Pearson Education.

Brown, H. D., & Lee, H. (2015). *Teaching by principles: An interactive approach to pedagogy* (4th ed.). White Plains, NY: Pearson Education.

Canale, M., & Swain, M. (1980). Theoretical bases of communicative approaches to second language teaching and testing. *Applied Linguistics, 1*(1), 1–47.

Christiansen, T. (2011). *Cohesion: A discourse perspective.* Bern, Switzerland: Peter Lang.

Dirksen, C., & Smith, M. (2002). *Educator's English.* Changchun, China: Northeast Normal University Press.

Doughty, C., & Pica, T. (1986). Information gap tasks: Do they facilitate second language acquisition? *TESOL Quarterly, 20*(2), 305–325.

Gass, S. M. (1997). *Input, interaction, and the second language learner.* Mahwah, NJ: Lawrence Erlbaum.

Harmer, J. (2015). *The practice of English language teaching* (5th ed.). Essex, England: Pearson Education.

Hendrickson, J. M. (1980). Error correction in foreign language teaching: Recent theory, research and practice. In K. Croft (Ed.), *Readings on English as a second language* (2nd ed.). Cambridge, MA: Winthrop Publishers.

Hinkel, E. (Ed.). (2011). *Handbook of research in second language teaching and learning* (Vol. 2, pp. 593–610). New York, NY: Routledge.

Hinkel, E. (Ed.). (2019). *Teaching essential units of language: Beyond single-word vocabulary.* New York, NY: Routledge.

Hofstede, G. (1980). *Culture's consequences: International differences in work-related values.* Beverly Hills, CA: Sage Publications.

Hughes, R. (2010). *Materials to develop the speaking skills.* In N. Harwood (Ed.), *English language teaching materials: Theory and practice* (pp. 207–224). New York, NY: Cambridge.

Jenkins, J. (2006). Current perspectives on teaching World Englishes and English as a lingua franca. *TESOL Quarterly, 40*(1), 157–181.

Lightbown, P. M., & Spada, N. (2013). How languages are learned (4th ed.). Oxford, England: Oxford University Press.

Long, M. (1983). Native speaker/non-native speaker conversation and the negotiation of comprehensible input. *Applied Linguistics, 4*(2), 126–141.

Lyster, R., & Ranta, L. (1997). Corrective feedback and learner uptake: Negotiations of form in communicative classrooms. *Studies in Second Language Acquisition, 19*(1), 37–61.

Lyster, R., Saito, K., & Sato, M. (2013). Oral corrective feedback in second language classrooms. *Language Teaching, 46*(1), 1–40. doi:10.1017///S0261444812000365.

Mey, J. L. (2001). *Pragmatics: An introduction.* Malden, MA: Blackwell Publishers.

Nation, I. S. P. (2011). Second language speaking. In E. Hinkel (Ed.), *Handbook of research in second language teaching and learning* (Vol. 2, pp. 444–454). New York, NY: Routledge.

Nation, I. S. P., & Newton, J. (2009). *Teaching ESL/EFL listening and speaking.* New York, NY: Routledge.

Otheguy, R., Garcia, O., & Reid, W. (2015). Clarifying translanguaging and deconstructing named languages: A perspective from linguistics. *Applied Linguistics Review, 6*(3), 281–307. doi:http://dx.doi.org/10.1515/applirev-2015-0014.

Pink, D. H. (2009). *Drive: The surprising truth about what motivates us.* New York, NY: Riverhead Books.

Richards, J. C. (2006). *Communicative language teaching today.* New York, NY: Cambridge.

Richards, J. (2017). *Curriculum development in language teaching* (2nd ed.). New York, NY: Cambridge University Press.

Savignon, S. J. (2005). *Communicative language teaching: Strategies and goals.* In E. Hinkel (Ed.), *Handbook of research in second language teaching and learning* (pp. 635–651). Mahwah, NJ: Lawrence Erlbaum.

Selinker, L. (1972). Interlanguage. *International Review of Applied Linguistics, 10*(3), 209–231.

Sheen, Y., & Ellis, R. (2011). Corrective feedback in language teaching. In E. Hinkel (Ed.), *Handbook of research in second language teaching and learning* (Vol. 2, pp. 593–610). New York, NY: Routledge.

Yule, G. (1996). *Pragmatics*. Oxford, England: Oxford University Press.

Appendix:
Sample Lesson Plan

Moving From Mechanical to Meaningful to Communicative: Talking About the Past

Resources

- Whiteboard or blackboard and writing utensil
- Dice roll question sheets
- Dice (one die per pair of students)
- Blank survey sheets
- Lesson objectives

Upon completion of this lesson, students will be able to

- Ask questions in simple past tense using the correct grammatical structure.
- Create simple past-tense sentences in both the affirmative and negative.
- Extend a conversation in the past tense for more than 3 minutes.

Warm-Up

Introduce the focus on the past by sharing a short story from when you were a child. Ask students what tenses were used during the story.

Opening Discussion

In pairs, have students review past tense by asking them to come up with the rules for making negative past-tense sentences. Have the pairs discuss: How do you make a negative sentence in the past tense?

Review with students: To make a negative past-tense sentence, just add *did not* (or *didn't*) before the verb. The past tense of the *be* verbs (*am*, *is*, and *are*) are *was* and *were*. To make them negative, you just add *not*. (I *wasn't* sick. They *weren't* tired.)

Positive	Negative
I went	I didn't go
You swam	You didn't swim
We ate	We didn't eat
They sat	They didn't sit
He gave	He didn't give
She climbed	She didn't climb
It jumped	It didn't jump

Speaking Practice Drill with a Die

Give pairs of students one die and a handout with past-tense questions (see Roll a Die; Ask a Question). The first student will roll the die and his or her partner will ask the number of the question he or she rolls. If you roll a 1, answer A1. If the student roles a 1 a second time, her or she should answer question B1 and so on. Remind students to say more than *yes* or *no*! For example, the students could say, "Yes. I learned English as a child at school. My first English class was in first grade." Students continue to roll the die and answer questions until all the questions have been answered or the teacher stops them.

Roll a Die; Ask a Question

Take turns rolling the die. The first student will roll the die and the other person will ask the number of the question he or she rolls. If you roll a 1, answer A1. The next time you roll a 1, answer B1. Answer with 1 or 2 sentences, not just *yes* or *no*! Let the next person roll and continue the activity.

A

1. Did you learn English as a child?
2. Did you eat breakfast this morning?
3. Did you leave your house at 8 a.m.?
4. Did you buy bread last week?
5. Did you ride the bus to school?
6. Did you sit in the same seat this week as last week?

B

1. Did you walk to the store last month?
2. Did you call someone last week?
3. Did you buy fruit yesterday?
4. Did you grow up in Africa?
5. Did you find an apartment?
6. Did you eat Mexican food last night?

C

1. Did you get a gift for your birthday?
2. Did you forget to do your homework?
3. Did you swim in a lake as a child?
4. Did you drive a car in your home country?
5. Did you feel tired last week?
6. Did you have a good time on your last holiday?

D

1. Did you sleep poorly last night?

2. Did you take Main Street to school?

3. Did you wear a jacket yesterday?

4. Did you write an email to your family last week?

5. Did you sing on Sunday?

6. Did you see a movie last week?

Survey Part I

Students write three of their own questions that start with *did* and focus on childhood. For example, did you play soccer as a child?

Survey Part II

Students ask three classmates to answer their questions and record those classmates' answers in the chart.

Question	Person 1	Person 2	Person 3
1.			
2.			
3.			

Survey Part III

In pairs, students summarize the answers of their three classmates. Remind students to answer in full sentences (e.g., Jane rode a bike as a child, but she did not play soccer).

Teaching Speaking

Keeping a Conversation Going

Review strategies on how to keep a conversation going with the whole class. See chapter 2 of this book for ideas.

Discussion

In trios, hold a discussion using the provided questions. Remember to be aware of past-tense verbs. Find ways to keep the conversation going so that all three people speak at least two times.

- What did you like to do when you were a child?
- What is the most unusual thing that you have done (since coming to this country, starting college, etc.)?
- What languages have you studied?
- What is different between last year and this year?

After-Class Work

Have students interview two friends or family members about their childhoods. They should take careful notes and be prepared to share stories from their family or friends with classmates in the next lesson.